ODDBALL SAYINGS, WITTY EXPRESSIONS & DOWN HOME FOLKLORE

A Collection of Clever Phrases

MIRIAM C. LARSEN

R & E PUBLISHERS

D1707354

R & E Publishers

468 Auzerais Ave., Suite A, San Jose, CA 95126 Tel: (408) 977-0691

Oddball Sayings, Witty Expressions and Down Home Folklore:
***A Collection of Clever Phrases*   by Miriam Larsen**

Book Design, Typesetting and Illustrations by Kaye Quinn/Kaye Graphics
Cover design by Joseph E. Haga and Smart Design

Library of Congress Cataloging-in-Publication Data

Oddball Sayings, Witty Expressions and Down Home Folklore:
A Collection of Clever Phrases [compiled] by Miriam C. Larsen.

    p.   cm.
ISBN 1-56875-077-3 : $6.95
1. Aphorisms and apothegms. 2. Proverbs, American. 3. American wit and humor. 4. American wit and humor, Pictorial. I. Larsen, Miriam C. II. Title: Oddball Sayings, Witty Expressions & Down Home Folklore.
PN6271.W67   1994   93-43757
082 .0207--dc20   CIP

Ellen,
Thanks for your contribution. Send me some more and I'll do another edition.
Love,
Miriam

Dedicated to all those who contributed and to everyone who reads it.

Miriam C. Larson

INTRODUCTION

Several years ago, friends of mine, Vera Mae and Bailey Harris, of Van Alstyne, Texas, told me that if it rains on the first day of the month, it will rain fifteen days during that month. I marked my calendar, and sure enough, it rained fifteen days during that month.

From then on I began hearing sayings from other people, and I started writing them down. I also asked everyone I know, and some I don't, to add to what I had collected. This book contains sayings from people scattered all over the globe.

If it rains on the first day of the month, it will rain 15 days during the same month.

If the sun is shining when it rains, it will rain at the same time next day.

Two times around the thumb equals the wrist; two times around the wrist equals the neck; two times around the neck equals the waist.

A person so ugly they'll stop a 9-day clock.

Beggars can't be choosers.

Taking bread when you already have some means some hungry person is coming to visit.

Anything that is planted in the shadow of the moon, won't freeze.

Dream of a wedding, there will be a death.

Red sky in the morning - sailors beware, red sky at night - sailors delight.

A rut is a grave with both ends knocked out.

Wear clean underwear. What if you get hit by a car and have to go to the hospital?

Don't eat yellow snow.

Beauty is as beauty does.

If you lie down with dogs, don't be surprised if you get up with fleas.

It's amazing how our children marry worthless, dumb, ugly mates, but they produce the most brilliant, handsome/pretty children.

A stitch in time saves nine..

Rain on Monday, rain three days during the week.

Rain on Easter Sunday, rain for seven Sundays.

Find a pin and pick it up, all the day you will have good luck.

The proof of the cook is in the pudding.

Once bitten, twice shy.

When a cat sleeps on it's back, it will rain.

If a caterpillar has a narrow band around it's middle,
we are in for a hard winter.

Rain before 7:00, shine before 11:00.

If you tell your dream before breakfast, it will come true.

If you step on a crack, you'll break your mother's back.

If you sit on a feather pillow in a thunderstorm, lightning won't strike you.

If a black cat crosses your path, you will have bad luck
if you don't cross your fingers and change your route.

If a fisherman spits on his hook and names it someone special, he will catch a big fish.

If you drink a tablespoon of dill pickle juice, you can get rid of the hiccups.

A morning rain is like an old lady's dance, soon over.

If you can pinch more than an inch at your waist, you need to lose weight.

If a pregnant woman carries her baby high, it will be a girl. If she carries it low, it will be a boy.

Three color cats are female.

Fleas are gone after the first freeze.

If you play with a frog, warts will appear on your hands.

If it rains on your wedding day, you will have years of unhappiness.

Place your thumb against your index finger. That's how long your nose is.

Food fantasies: Eat green olives for passion; carrots for good eyes; onions for good nerves; two spoons of honey each morning - no arthritis; raisins for good blood.

After leaving home, if you must go back to get something, sit down and count to ten before leaving again.

When walking with someone and a post comes between you, an argument will ensue.

An apple a day keeps the doctor away.

Drinking milk while eating fish will make you sick.

If you sprinkle salt on a bird's tail, the bird can't fly.

If your right eye itches, you will have guests.

Put the pedal to the metal.

I'll be a monkey's uncle.

If smoke lays close to the ground, bad weather is coming.

A man of words and not of deeds is like a garden filled with weeds.

Beware of a man who is cruel to his mother.

He didn't fall off no turnip truck.

A dog that barks, won't bite.

If you find a penny, you will have good luck.

What goes up always comes down.

One rotten apple can spoil a whole bushel.

There is not a pot that's crooked that there isn't a lid that fits.

If your right hand itches, you are going to meet a stranger.

Death comes in threes.

A rolling stone gathers no moss.

A soft answer turns away anger.

A piece of raw bacon on a boil will heal it.

Put snuff or tobacco juice on a wasp or bee sting, and it will not hurt.

A black cat has one white hair.

If you bend over and look at the moon upside down through your legs, the moon will appear much smaller.

A cricket on the hearth is a sign of good luck.

He is so crooked he'd steal the eyeballs out of your head and then swear he paid $500 for them.

I'm so mad I could kill him and tell God he died.

Cooler than a cucumber.

Ask no questions, and I'll tell you no lies.

Cold hands - warm heart.

Pretty is as pretty does.

Beauty is only skin deep.

You can't beat out of the flesh what's in the bones.

Love at first sight is like a lightning flash during the night.

Rags to riches in three generations.

Her elevator doesn't go all the way to the top.

So cold it was a three dog night.

Faster than a herd of turtles.

Don't look a gift horse in the mouth.

Never bite off more than you can chew.

He couldn't hit a bull with a bass fiddle.

Clumsy as a bull in a china closet.

Poor as a church mouse.

Mad as a wet hen.

I'm going to turn over every stone.

Kill a black snake and hang it in a tree, it will rain in 24 hours.

A clean ship is a happy ship.

Busy hands are happy hands.

He who hesitates is lost.

A new broom sweeps clean.

The coffee is so strong, you can chew it.

This coffee could float a horseshoe.

This coffee can walk by itself.

Her hips are two ax handles wide.

I wouldn't have him/her if he/she was made of solid gold.

There's no fool like an old fool.

You sleep best with your bed facing east.

Snakes will not bite cats.

You can hypnotize a chicken by putting it's beak on a string.

Till hell freezes over.

The rain was a frog strangler.

You can lead a horse to water but you can't make him drink.

He is so ugly he looks like his face caught on fire and it was put out with an ax.

He is meaner than a junk yard dog.

Can't find a needle in a haystack.

He is so stupid he can't pour beer out of a boot.

With those teeth he can eat a persimmon through a fence.

I've never liked hot beer or cold coffee.

Must have been slapped by a haint.

When there is smoke, there is fire.

What goes around comes around.

A cat always knows when an earthquake is going to occur.

Never put a hat on a bed. If you do bad luck is sure to follow.

Never bring a hoe or a rake into the house.

Never start a plane or train trip on Friday.

Always make a cross in the road and spit into it if you must turn around and retrace your steps.

If you should spill salt, throw a pinch of it over your right shoulder for good luck.

If you find a coin in the street, always keep it for good luck.

To prevent a storm, stick an ax into the ground to split the cloud.

Wearing an undergarment wrong side out will bring bad luck.

Carry a rabbit's foot for good luck.

Never open an umbrella inside the house.

If the sun shines while it is raining, the devil is whipping his wife.

If you drop a dish cloth while drying dishes, guests are sure to come calling.

If you were born in the AM, you are a night person. If you were born in the PM, you are a day person.

When your left eye itches, you will be happy. If your right eye itches, sadness will follow.

When your left hand itches, you will receive money. When your right hand itches, you will lose money.

When you see a load of hay make a wish and never look back, and say, "Load of hay, load of hay, take my wish and go away." Your wish will come true.

If you find a bone, make a wish and throw the bone over your shoulder.

When small birds or animals are in your path, spit to ward off evil spirits.

Always go out the same door you entered.

Fade the heat and handle the grief.

People die within a span of 45 days of their birthday.

If you can't sleep, you have a guilty conscience.

When you find a pin with the point toward you, you will have good luck.

If your nose itches, someone will come with holes in their britches.

Knock on wood for good luck.

Never invite 13 people for dinner.

Wash face with dew to remove freckles.

Pregnant women should not witness ugly events because children are marked by what their mothers see, hear and do during their pregnancy.

Make sure a baby sneezes to rid it of evil spirits.

If your handwriting is large, you are secure. If your handwriting is small, you are insecure.

If a bird flies into the house, an important message is sure to come.

If you get a mole above your chin, you'll never be beholden to your kin.

A mole on your arm can do you no harm.

Touch blue and your wish will come true.

When two people reach for the same piece of bread, guests will be coming.

If a black cat comes to visit, it will bring good luck. If it stays, there will be bad luck.

Blow out the candles on your birthday cake with one puff and your wish will come true.

When skies are cloudy and enough blue appears in the sky to make a Dutch man a pair of pants, the skies will clear up.

That takes the rag off the bush.

Free advice is what it's worth - nothing.

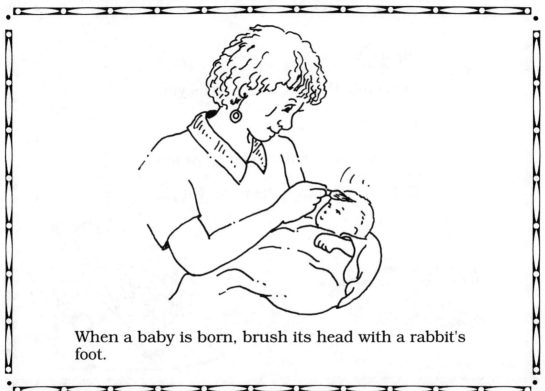

When a baby is born, brush its head with a rabbit's foot.

Sly as fox.

Don't bite the hand that feeds you.

Crazy like a fox.

Absence makes the heart grow fonder.

If the cat is away, the mice will play.

Marry in haste, repent in leisure.

A burned child dreads the fire.

Friday, the fairest of foulest.

Evening red and morning gray sends the traveler on his way.

Evening gray and morning red keeps the traveler home in bed.

A dog that will bring a bone will bury one.

He's anyone's coon dog that will hunt with him.

* *

Drunk as a skunk.

Stubborn as a mule

High tail it out of here.

He is a pompous ass.

Spry as a cricket.

Dull as a frog.

Sharp as a tack.

I smell a rat.

* *

Two is a party, three is a crowd, four on the sidewalk not allowed.

The show is over and the monkey is dead.

If it ain't broke, don't fix it.

It's the best thing since the nickel cigar.

It's the best thing since sliced bread.

Crazy as a cut coon.

Wise as an owl.

He is lying like a dog.

Flat as a pancake.

Crooked as a barrel of snakes.

High as a kite.

Colder than a well digger's ass.

Good fences make good neighbors.

Guests and fish smell after three days.

Hotter than the hammers of hell.

Neat as a pin.

The grass is always greener on the other side of the fence.

Red as a beet.

Snug as a bug in a rug.

Sleep like a log.

Eating high on the hog.

Tall as a Georgia pine.

Curse like a sailor.

Easy as falling off a log.

Every dog has his day.

Sober as a judge.

Don't be a wet blanket.

Hot as a Saturday night six shooter.

Ants in your pants.

File your fingernails on Friday, cry before Sunday.

Busy as a bee.

Hungry as a bear.

Cheap as dirt.

Spinning like the knob on an outhouse door.

It looks good on paper.

He talks a good game.

Still water runs deep.

Blind as a bat.

Ugly as a mud fence.

When having a baby, put scissors under the bed to cut the pain.

Bright as a new penny.

Its raining cats and dogs.

Its raining pitchforks.

Its raining tadpoles.

Nutty as a fruitcake.

Over the fence is out.

Wild as a March hare.

Crazy as a loon.

The two joints in the middle finger measure an inch.

The best remedy for a short temper is a long walk.

To get rid of the corns on your toes, soak bread in vinegar, bind it on the toe day and night and the corn will come out by the roots.

When a person is choking, break an egg and give only the egg white to the person. The egg white will wrap around the obstacle and remove it.

If wishes were horses, beggars would ride.

After having a baby, put a needle between the mother's breasts to dry up the milk.

Give a newborn baby catnip tea so it will not break out with hives.

Many hotels do not have a 13th floor because it is bad luck.

When the wind is out of the east, fishing is least, when the wind is out of the west, fishing is best.

A red and yellow coral snake will kill a fellow, a yellow and black - venom lack.

It always thunders before lightning.

Put a rubber hose in fruit trees to keep the birds away.

Never get on a horse on the right side.

People who live in glass houses shouldn't throw stones.

Don't put all your eggs in one basket.

If there is a ring around the moon, it will rain.

If the big dipper is tipping, it will rain.

Birds of a feather all flock together.

The best cure for insomnia is Monday morning.

When a cat sleeps curled up with it's head turned chin uppermost, then rainy weather is due soon.

Pick and store winter fruit when the moon is full so it will retain its plumpness.

Lamb's tails should be docked during a waxing moon.

Dock a horse's tail so that a witch can't hold on to it.

A watched pot never boils.

When building a new house, avoid locations near gallows, suicide and murder sites.

Start building a new house when the moon is full.

Eyebrows that meet in the middle indicate a criminal mentality.

A mole on the chin indicates success.

A mole on the thigh indicates misfortune.

A mole on the right temple indicates wealth and a high position or office.

A bad penny always returns.

To deflect feelings of hate or ill will that are directed at you, make a witch bottle. Put nails, pins and pieces of broken glass in the bottle. Bury the bottle in the garden or under the front doorstep. All negativity will avoid you and be absorbed by the bottle.

Never turn a cat away from your door

If a dog howls three times in the night near a house containing a sick person, it is an omen of death.

A face pack made of pulped apples will keep the skin firm and ward off wrinkles.

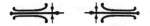

To get rid of a headache, visualize pulling the pain out on a piece of string and then throwing the string away.

Corns will gradually go away if they are cut in the waning moon.

To avoid nightmares, your bed should face east to west, never north to south.

Most births take place when the moon is changing.

It is hotter than nickel chili.

It is hotter than a depot stove.

When the sage brush has purple blooms, it will rain.

Thick as fleas.

Shirt-tail relatives.

If you sew on Sunday, you'll have to remove the stitches by Friday.

Lord willing and the creeks don't rise.

A heavy coat on an animal means bad weather.

When cattle lie down in the field, the weather will change.

It is bad luck to put your shoes higher than the floor.

If you have a child who wets the bed, put a pan of water under his bed and the wetting will stop.

If knives in the kitchen accidentally cross blades, this will bring bad luck. To negate this, pick them up vertically and tap their handles on a table top three times.

Convince a man against his will and he is of the same opinion still.

Predict rainy weather according to which tree comes into leaf first in Spring: Oak before Ash is just a splash. Ash before Oak is a real soak.

If you see a rook, it's a crow. If you see crows, they're rooks.

It is good luck if you spit when you see a white horse.

The way to a man's heart is through his stomach.

Her walk reminds me of the windshield wipers on a Ford pickup truck.

It is going to be a long dry spell.

It is bad luck to look at a full moon through glass.

A car without air-conditioning - four windows down and forty miles an hour.

The old gray mare ain't what it used to be.

Six of one, half dozen of the other

They treat me like a mushroom, keep me in the dark and feed me manure.

If it rains on St. Swithin's Day, it will rain forty days and forty nights.

It is bad luck to walk under a ladder without crossing your fingers.

Why kick a dead horse?

Why close the barn door after the horse is out?

You can lead a horse to water but you can't make him drink.

Double a three year old child's height and you will have his height as an adult.

Dull women have immaculate houses.

When all else fails, read the directions.

You're not fat until people jump over you rather than walk around you.

A career woman has to look like a lady, act like a man, and work like a dog.

Drop a fork - a man will visit. Drop a spoon - a woman will visit.

He is two sheets to the wind.

Rougher than a stucco bathtub.

Never trust a skinny cook.

One second - the time it takes for the stop light to turn green and the car behind you to honk.

If there is dew on the grass in the morning, it will not rain that day.

Long about lightning bug time, gonna pour down rain.

He is one sandwich short of a picnic.

He is not paddling with two oars.

A seamstress never uses a long thread.

My forgetter worked overtime.

Nervous as a whore in church.

100 years from now, we won't know the difference.

Candy is dandy, but liquor is quicker.

Lips that touch liquor will never touch mine.

There may be snow on the roof top, but there's fire in the furnace.

When you say something bad about someone then someone may be talking about you.

Put a silver dollar in a baby's hand. If the hand is squeezed, the baby will grow up frugal. If the hand is not squeezed, the baby will grow up to be a big spender.

Women - if the wrist measures 4 1/2 inches, you are small boned, 5 1/2 inches, you are medium boned, 6 1/2 inches, you are large boned.

Happy as a pig in a mud hole.

You think of yourself as 20 years younger than you are.
You think being old is 20 older than you are.

Dear Reader:

    Do you have any favorite sayings you would like to add? If so, send them to me at the following address. Who knows, the Publisher may insist on a second edition.

MIRIAM C. LARSEN
714 Sceptre Circle
Garland, TX. 75043

About the Author

Miriam C. Larsen grew up in Galesburg, Illinois. After receiving a journalism degree from Harding University in Searcy, Arkansas, she settled in Texas. Miriam does not want to be remembered as only the author of *Wise...Or OtherWise Information & Sayings*. Her other books include: *The Midas Touch*, the story of Beatrice Food Companies, Inc.; *57,000 Sunsets*, the story of Galesburg, Illinois; and *Where Are The Psychics?*, an international directory. Miriam is listed in *Who's Who in the South and Southwest*, *Who's Who of American Women*, *The World Who's Who of Women*, and the *Directory of International Biography*.

GET MORE FUN BOOKS FROM R&E PUBLISHERS

TITLE	ORDER #	PRICE
Oddball Sayings, Witty Expressions & Down Home Folklore *by Miriam Larsen*	077-3	$6.95
Death is...Lighthearted Views of a Grave Situation *by Rich Hillman & Steven Mickle*	965-2	$7.95
101 Uses for a Dead IRS Agent... *by Don Hipschman & James Waltz*	975-X	$7.95
Medisins Rx: Your Prescription to Laughter *by Craig Peterson*	963-6	$7.95
Revenge in the Classroom: Skool Kartoons for Everyone *by Kent Grimsley*	966-0	$9.95
Laffs from the Bottom of the Pit...The Musician's Joke Book...And for Conductors too! *by Susan Nigro* Regular Version	930-X	$5.95
Adult Version	921-0	$5.95
More Laffs from the Bottom of the Pit...The Musician's Joke Book... And for Conductors too! *by Susan Nigro*	082-X	$6.95
Retirement and Other Myths: Musings on the Leisurely Life with a Dash of Humor & Advice *by Elliott Richman*	074-9	$9.95

YOUR ORDER

ORDER #	QTY	UNIT PRICE	TOTAL PRICE

Please rush me the following books. I want to save by ordering three books and receive FREE shipping charges. Orders under 3 books please include $2.50 shipping. California residents add 8.25% tax.

YOUR ADDRESS

Name: _____

Organization: _____

Address: _____

City/State/Zip: _____

PAYMENT METHOD

☐ Enclosed check or money order

☐ MasterCard Card Expires_____ Signature_____

☐ Visa

R & E Publishers • 468 Auzerais Ave., Suite A, San Jose, CA 95126 Tel: (408) 977-0691